The MORK & MINDY STORY™

by Peggy Herz

SCHOLASTIC BOOK SERVICES

NEW YORK • TORONTO • LONDON • AUCKLAND • SYDNEY • TOKYO

Henderson Production Company, Inc. and Miller-Milkis Productions, Inc. in association with Paramount Television present *Mork & Mindy*. Created by Garry K. Marshall, Dale McRaven, and Joe Glauberg. "The Flying Egg" based upon "Mork: Hour Special" written by Dale McRaven.

ISBN: 0-590-05756-1

12 11 10 9 8 7 6 5 4   9/7 0 1 2 3 4/8

Contents

It's a bird . . . it's a plane . . . it's an egg?? Actually, Mork from Ork has just landed on Earth, with his luggage carefully tucked away in a big, white egg.

The Flying Egg

One night, a big white egg came drifting down to Earth from out of the sky. It settled down gently in a field of trees and green grass. Then a very strange thing happened, for this was no ordinary flying egg. This was a landing vehicle from outer space. It carried a passenger who had been sent to Earth on a very important mission.

The egg shook and bounced around and then it cracked wide open. Out stepped a strange-looking creature in a far-out space suit. Earthlings didn't know it yet, but they had just been invaded by a one-man force from a planet 60 million light years away. Mork from Ork had arrived.

Moments after Mork had stepped out onto the surface of Earth, another egg settled down into the grass beside him. Mork had been expecting it. He cracked open the second egg and pulled out his suitcase. Then he looked back into the egg and discovered that interplanetary space travel isn't all that it's cracked up to be. "Only one!" he cried in disgust to the yolkless egg. "You lost half my luggage!"

Half was better than none, however, for Mork had landed near Boulder, Colorado, and he had been told to blend in with his surroundings. And even Orkans know that your average man-about-town in Boulder, Colorado, just isn't wearing space suits and helmets. So Mork changed quickly into more proper Earthling attire.

The outfit didn't make much sense to him, but he knew he would catch on to the strange ways of the people on this planet called Earth. He slipped his arms into the sleeves of the coat jacket and buttoned it down his back. Then he tied his tie and hung it down his back too. Now nobody would ever know that he was an alien. He was ready to carry out his assignment.

Orson had been very clear about that assignment. Orson had sent him from Ork to learn all he could about the primitive living conditions on Earth. Orson had also wanted to get Mork off Ork. "You constantly make jokes," Orson had told him. "You call me Fatso behind my back.

...You painted a mustache on the solar lander.... That just won't do."

So he sent Mork to Earth, and Mork was happy to go. Mork had been on Earth before and he had liked it. That time, he had landed in Milwaukee, Wisconsin, where he had met Fonzie and Richie Cunningham.

Now, he was back, and he was going to stay a while. He would learn everything he could and report it all back to his leader on Ork. He was ready to begin. He stepped away from the egg that had brought him to Earth and moved off through the trees.

He had not gone far when he met his first Earthling of the trip. He didn't know it then, but her name was Mindy, and she was to play an important part in his mission on this planet. When he met her, she was standing all alone, looking around angrily. She had arrived in this spot by automobile — her own — and then her boyfriend had driven off in it, leaving her stranded.

She was happy to see Mork. She didn't know his jacket was on backward. She thought he was a priest.

Mork walked Mindy back to her apartment, and she offered him a glass of iced tea. And then...she began to notice things about Mork.

They were small things, perhaps, but they added up....

Mork put his hand in the glass of iced tea and drank it through his fingers.

Mindy asked him to sit down, and he did. On his head.

There was a noise at the door and Mindy opened it. There sat a big white egg. "My lost luggage," Mork explained cheerfully.

Mork asked Mindy if he might take her picture. She agreed. He held up his gloved hand and snapped the picture. "Instamatic glove," he told her.

Finally, Mindy said, "You're not a priest. Who are you?" Mork had never learned to lie.

"I'm Mork from Ork," he answered calmly.

Mindy screamed a bit ("Is that your way of saying thanks?" Mork asked innocently), but Mindy — without knowing it — was already committed to her new alien friend. She didn't understand him. She had no idea where Ork was. Mork tried to tell her about his planet and his life there.

He'd grown up without parents, he explained. "I'm a test tube baby," he said. "My father ran off with a bottle of nose drops."

Did it make any sense? No, it didn't. Not to Mindy or to anyone else. But Mindy couldn't turn her guest away. She agreed to let him stay in the attic of her apartment. He was like a friendly puppy who needed a home, only he was anything but a puppy. He was an Orkan, but he could think and act and speak like an Earthling. Only sometimes he did all of those things very, very...strangely.

If he was going to get along on Earth, he would need help — lots and lots of help. Mindy agreed to help him, but she had one big worry. She didn't want her father to find out that there was an alien living in her attic. Her father was very nice and all that, but, somehow...she just knew he wouldn't understand. How do you explain to your own father about someone who arrives in a big white egg — with his luggage following behind him in another big white egg? It would sound like one big yolk. Er...joke. And Mindy's father just might not laugh.

Mork tried hard to fit in. It wasn't easy. One day Mindy's father discovered Mork was living in Mindy's attic. He sent a policeman to talk to him. Mindy's father wanted Mork out of the apartment.

"Take off," said the cop, trying to sound threatening.

"Take off? I just landed!" answered Mork, and the cop decided he was crazy. Absolutely bonkers.

"I had to take him in," the cop later told Mindy's father. "They're going to have a sanity hearing tomorrow. I'm afraid they're going to put him away."

Put Mork away? Even Mindy's father didn't want that. He didn't know (yet) that Mork was an alien, but he knew that things had gone too far! He and Mindy rushed to the sanity hearing to defend Mork.

The doctor who had examined Mork was beside himself. "He tried to put a square peg in a round hole," he cried to the judge.

"And I did it!" replied Mork, pulling up the leg of his pants and looking at the watch on his ankle.

"You see?" said the doctor, looking slightly crazy himself. "He's wearing a wristwatch on his ankle!"

"No, your honor," said Mork with his innocent smile. "I'm wearing an ankle watch on my ankle!" A true and logical statement; who could deny it? Not the judge; but he did know he had met someone unusual. He let Mork off, admitting as he did so that: "This defendant may add a new dimension to the word eccentric."

Mork, more than anybody else, learned something from that experience. He tried to tell Orson about it when he made his report back to Ork. "Everybody on this planet is an individual and *proud* of it!" he said, still surprised by everything

Mork has shed his spacesuit for some down-to-earth clothes — but Mindy's dad has a definite feeling he's just met someone a little "out of this world!"

that he had observed on Earth. "And, Orson, I met a girl...she came to the hearing. She defied the system to defend me.

"Orson," Mork added, "knowing someone would do this makes me feel good inside."

Orson listened to Mork's report, but then he gave him a strict warning. "You're there to observe, not to get involved," he cautioned the young space traveler.

Mork has never found it easy to follow that advice, however. From the moment he arrived on Earth, he has gotten involved, often without meaning to. And ever since he first stepped out of that egg, Mork has involved millions of Earthlings in his life too. For the TV audience, a

7

hit was hatched when that egg cracked open. And the golden center of the hit is an Orkan who looks at us through different eyes — and sees us more clearly than we see ourselves. He has turned *Mork and Mindy* into the biggest new comedy hit of the year. And he has made it look easy and spontaneous.

Making a TV show into a big comedy hit isn't easy; it takes talent and time and hard work. It also takes luck — and luck was with the producers of *Mork and Mindy* when they were casting the show. They hired someone to play Mork in an episode in *Happy Days*, but the actor they had hired changed his mind. The producers had to replace him quickly. They held an open audition, and a young comic actor came walking in off the street. Nobody knew him. His name, he said, was Robin Williams.

Robin Williams:
Voted "Funniest" and
"Least Likely to Succeed"

Morkomania began about a year ago. Until then, most normal Earthlings weren't twisting their ears or chirping "Na-no, na-no" at each other. Now they are.

Morkomania actually began because of nine-year-old Scotti Marshall. Scotti was a big *Star Wars* fan. He was also a big *Happy Days* fan. *Happy Days*, he decided, needed a sci-fi touch. How about a visitor from outer space? An alien in Milwaukee?

Scotti took the idea to the producer of the show. It wasn't any big deal. He didn't even have to make an appointment to see the producer, in fact, for the producer happened to be his dad, Garry Marshall.

Garry Marshall is one of TV's most successful

producers. He played a major role in the creation and development of *Happy Days*. Then he introduced two young women on *Happy Days* and later gave them their own show. They were *Laverne and Shirley*. Soon, their popularity topped even that of the Cunningham clan.

In the spring of 1978, Marshall introduced his alien in an episode of *Happy Days*. He called him Mork from Ork. Mork came to Richie Cunningham one night in a dream. Or was it a dream? Richie didn't think so — and he was right! For Mork came back to Earth later and he even revisited Milwaukee, where Fonzie fixed him up on a date with Laverne.

Mork wasn't quite ready for the date, however. He hadn't learned enough about how real Earthlings act. Laverne thought he was really weird. She was very angry with Fonzie for fixing her up with Mork. "Fonz," she said in disgust, "I washed my hair for this! I ironed my skirt!" Mork just stood and smiled, understanding very little of what was going on.

Garry Marshall never intended to make Mork the star of his own series. Mork was to be in one episode of *Happy Days* and that was all. But TV viewers of all ages had something to say about that. They said it in cards and letters which poured into the network and the TV studio.

Network executives scratched their heads.

Who could predict the tastes of the viewing public? Only one thing was clear: People wanted more of Mork. Could a one-shot appearance be turned into a weekly series? Garry Marshall said he would try. He knew he already had one big thing going for him in Robin Williams.

Marshall had originally picked comedian John Byner to play Mork in the *Happy Days* episode, but Byner had begged off at the last minute.

Enter Robin Williams.

But who was Robin Williams?

I met Robin for the first time in May of 1978. I had seen him in the *Happy Days* episode, but I knew very little about him. I met him for lunch at a restaurant in Los Angeles. Robin ordered a sandwich — a tuna melt (tuna and melted cheese), and looked with interest at the people around us.

No one paid any attention to us. Millions of TV viewers had seen Robin playing Mork on *Happy Days*, but none of the other customers seemed to recognize him. That kind of attention was still several months off.

My first meeting with Robin Williams was quite an event. He was wearing his favorite clothes—baggy pants, a bright T-shirt, and colorful suspenders.

He was soon to go into production for the *Mork and Mindy* series, and then he had no idea what would happen in the next few months.

During our first meeting, Robin talked enthusiastically about his new series — and the new life that was beginning for him. The following week, he told me, he was going to be married in an outdoor ceremony in Tiburon, California, outside San Francisco. He was marrying a dancer and choreographer named Valerie Velardi.

I liked Robin immediately. He is a warm, friendly, intelligent person. He has a wacky sense of humor and a wild imagination. Just how wild, I didn't fully understand when I first met him. But I found out a short time later.

"I have a slight Scottish accent," Robin told me then. "That's because I was born in Scotland and lived there for a year as a child."

Right. I wrote it all down. I believed it. Then I began to read the things he was telling other people in later interviews. "I was born in Detroit," he told one interviewer. "I was born in Chicago," he told another one.

The next time I saw him, I asked him for the true story, and he just laughed cheerfully. So where was Robin Williams born? Probably Chicago, but maybe not. Maybe Detroit. Maybe Scotland. Maybe...Ork?

No matter where he was born, he is an actor and a comedian of enormous talent. I did find out that his father was an executive of the Ford

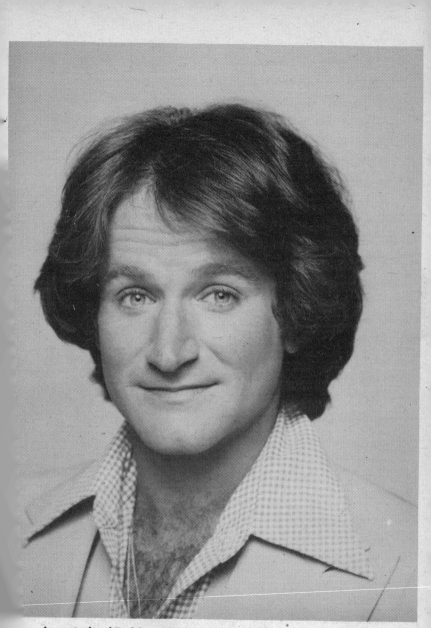

A portrait of Robin Williams. This brilliantly talented actor and comedian has won the hearts of TV viewers everywhere with his zany portrayal of Mork from Ork.

Motor Company, and Robin grew up as an only child. His two half brothers were already grown by the time he came along, and Robin spent much of his childhood alone, creating characters in his imagination.

"My father was moved around a great deal," Robin told me. "We moved back and forth between Chicago and Detroit three times. I went to junior high school in Lake Forest, Illinois, and in Birmingham, Michigan. During all that time, my imagination was my best friend."

When Robin was in high school, his father retired and the family moved to San Francisco. Robin loved that city. "I got moved ahead in school, though," he recalled, "and that was hard because I was still quite small when they moved me ahead. I wasn't involved in the high school drama department. I was into science and cross-country running. And I was concentrating on getting into college."

But San Francisco is a city that is proud of its arts and music and theater, and Robin discovered something there that he loved. "I started going to a place called The Committee, where young comics tried out their acts," he said. "It fascinated me to watch them. I wasn't really thinking of doing comedy myself, but I loved watching the others do it."

Robin was voted "Funniest" and "Least Likely to Succeed" by his high school classmates. With a send-off like that, how could he miss? He enrolled at Claremont Men's College, where he planned to major in political science. He lasted only one year, however, for he had gotten more and more involved with acting.

"My father was very worried," Robin admitted. "He saw my interests drifting toward the theater and he wondered how I could make a living in it. He urged me to take up a second profession like welding. But my father didn't try to stop me from doing whatever I wanted to do. He knew what it was to have a dream. But he wanted me to be practical about it."

Robin's first appearance as Mork was in an episode of Happy Days. Here he amazes the Fonz with some Orkan antics.

After Robin left Claremont, he enrolled at the College of Marin to study Shakespeare, as a literary course. That was better than political science (or welding), he discovered, but it still wasn't what he wanted to do. He wanted to study acting. And no matter how much he loved San Francisco, that wasn't the place to begin his career. It was time, he decided, to go to New York.

A Hit TV Show
— and a Lizard
Under the Refrigerator

Each year, thousands of young people pour into New York City. They come from all over the country, with fresh faces and high hopes.

They come because they want to be writers, artists, actors, musicians. And they choose New York because the city, in spite of its problems, is still the creative capital of the country. It has attracted many of the world's finest performers, writers, artists, and teachers. It offers some of the country's best schools. It has Broadway and off-Broadway, the New York Philharmonic, Lincoln Center, and the Metropolitan Museum of Art.

New York is the place where young people bring their dreams. They work and study and struggle and some become successful — if they're talented and lucky.

But what about Robin Williams? How — and why — did he decide to pursue *his* dream in New York?

Robin's father was a wealthy, successful businessman. Robin grew up in relative luxury. But that didn't mean his life was easy. Before he entered high school, he went to a private all-boys school. "I was fat and I used to get beaten up a lot," he recalled. "They called me 'dwarf' and 'leprechaun.' I started wrestling and dieted off 30 pounds in a year. The comedy started then."

And once it started, he couldn't stop it. He had tried college, but that didn't work. Finally, he won a scholarship to the famous Juilliard School in New York. Maybe he could do it, and maybe he couldn't, but he had to give it a try. The budding young actor had to see if he could make it in New York.

The Juilliard School offers training in all kinds of performing arts. The school teaches its acting students how to speak, sing, move, and do everything else that is part of acting. "I took everything there," Robin told me enthusiastically. "Juggling, gymnastics, mask work — everything. It was really super! I also became addicted to improvisational theater workshops. That led me, eventually, to doing stand-up comedy.

"Juilliard paid my tuition, but I had to pay my

room and board and it was tough at times. A bunch of us lived together. We ate a lot of cottage cheese, yogurt, and American Cheese sandwiches."

Robin didn't think of himself as "suffering for my craft," he said. "I was just trying to stay alive!"

He and a friend found one way to make money, however. They started performing mime in Central Park in New York City. (Mime is a way of acting without speaking, and just using movement.) Every day, they painted their faces white, put on rainbow suspenders and crazy costumes, and headed for the park.

"People stopped to watch us perform, and then we passed a hat at the end," Robin remembered. "Sometimes I made more than $100 a day. We performed in front of the Metropolitan Museum. The cops would try to move us on, but they weren't too strict. I don't think they allow performances there anymore, though."

Robin worked hard at Juilliard and he learned a lot there. But he discovered something when he got out. "Once you leave Juilliard and start looking for jobs," he told me, "it doesn't make much difference that you went there. Casting directors and others just want to see what you can do. Or it may even work against you if people feel you are too well-trained. Juilliard wants to train you well.

They want you to sound crisper than you did before — and there may be times when it is a disadvantage to speak well."

Robin's real voice does reflect his years of speech training. (But, then, it can also reflect a Scottish accent from that place where he *wasn't* born, or a Russian accent, or just about any other kind of accent. It's doubtful that he learned how to do all those accents at Juilliard!)

Robin left Juilliard in 1976 and went home to San Francisco. "I wanted to get into an acting company," he said, "but there was only one, and they weren't holding auditions right then. So I had to wait, and one night, I went to a comedy workshop. I started to work there regularly."

He worked there and he learned there, but he didn't get paid. "So I took other jobs to support myself," he said. "I worked as a waiter, as a house painter, and so on.

"In the workshop, we'd have classes and perform for each other. Then we'd start performing for the public. Since then, I have performed in many clubs, and I still don't get paid in many of them. The club figures it's doing you a favor by letting you perform. Maybe there will be an agent in the audience, they say — and sometimes there is!"

Robin grinned and shook his head. "I've really been in some awful places," he admitted. "I've performed in discos — while they were still dancing! I've been sandwiched between two rock 'n' roll bands... You just go through those times, telling yourself, 'I'll live,' and hoping you will. You just try to keep moving on to better and better clubs."

Robin kept moving and trying to improve his comedy routines. "You have to start finding your own style," he explained. "When I was a kid, I loved Jonathan Winters. I still do. He is my inspiration, but I've never met him.

"In my act, I do crazy characters with a lot of random madness. One of them is an old hippy poet called, Grandpa Funk. Another is Joey Stalin, a Russian stand-up comic. I use different

In this episode, a time machine turned Mork's age all the way back to three years old! Mindy watches closely as Mork has a temporary temper tantrum.

dialects and try to make each character different. I know a little Russian, but mainly I use Russian gibberish.

"I try to be as unique as possible in my comedy act," Robin said. "I don't write out my routines, but I write down concepts — or very general ideas."

Late last spring, Robin appeared before 7,000 people at a benefit concert in San Francisco. He loved the experience, he said enthusiastically. "Steve Martin was there and Joan Baez and others. We all did about 20-minute routines. I'd never performed before that many people before. It was really something. It was like performing in the Roman arena. Waves of laughter came at me. I guess I got a standing ovation. I couldn't be sure because there were so many people there."

The week before he tried out for the role of Mork in the *Happy Days* episode, Robin saw the movie, *Close Encounters of the Third Kind*. "After I saw that, I decided to add a new character to my act called the Alien Comedian," Robin told me with a laugh. "He talks gibberish. Then I walked in to read for Mork and the script called for Mork to use crazy sound effects — beeps, noises, etc. That's just what I had been doing in my act!"

It's ironic that Robin, a gentle, well-spoken

young man, got the role partially because he was good at talking gibberish and beeping. But that's show biz, as they say, and Robin has managed to combine the nonsense with more down-to-earth qualities of wonder, innocence, and humor in his portrayal of the Orkan named Mork.

It isn't hard to imagine Mork doing what Robin did — going to the park and entertaining children of all ages. Or standing, puzzled, trying to do a comedy act while the bands blared around him.

Being in a TV series — and having millions of viewers see you every week — can be a tremendous boost to anyone's career. Especially to the career of a relative unknown. And even though

It's a little bat-ty, but true! And Mindy is astounded when she finds Mork sleeping in true Orkan fashion — upside down, and next to his spacesuit!

he'd been working hard, Robin Williams was still an unknown when he was picked to play Mork. He loved playing him in the *Happy Days* episode. But to play him in a weekly series? Robin had some doubts.

"I didn't see how they could develop the character," Robin admitted in our first meeting. "But Garry Marshall assured me that everything would work out. He said we wouldn't be doing Shakespeare or any incredible drama, but that we would make the show as intelligent as possible, and we would give Mork two main characteristics: craziness and humanity. And we have done that."

Robin had done brief bits in the *Laugh-In* and *Richard Pryor* shows. "But I didn't really understand TV," he said, "until *Mork and Mindy* came along. It's not easy. My favorite thing is to improvise — to make up things as I go along, rather than following a prepared script. But the time limits of TV make that difficult to do. I manage to do some improvising, though," Robin added with his Morkan-like grin.

Even when the TV show is in production, Robin continues to perform at clubs in Los Angeles. "When this whole comedy thing works," he stressed, "it's wonderful. There are ups and downs to doing it. But the most important thing is to find new material and new ideas. A great excitement comes from finding new ideas that work.

"Comedy gives you a chance to really connect creatively. I'm still learning. Not too long ago, I was performing at a club and trying out new ideas — and I went on too long. I couldn't get myself off the stage. I wanted to leave, and the audience wanted me to leave. I don't write my act — and, that night, I just couldn't get myself off that stage."

Someday, Robin said, he'd like to have a number of things going on at once in his life — and he's getting close to that point right now with his comedy act and his TV show. "Now maybe a film," he said, "but I only want things to come to me as I'm ready for them."

And when he's not working? Is he a funnyman offstage, as well as on? "No," Robin replied. "I'm basically quiet when I'm offstage. Onstage — that's a time of high energy! When I'm not performing, I like to listen and watch everything going on around me. I love to read, run, body surf, roller skate — do all kinds of free-form physical activities. I love the beach in the summer. And I read a lot of science fiction. I also collect science fiction toys. Some of them are fantastic art! I've always been fascinated by science fiction."

Robin also loves going to movies, he said. "Especially old ones! And I enjoy going to animation festivals," he added. "Great things are being done in animation — and in music! I'd like to add music to my act someday. I'm taking piano now and starting to sing. So far, I sound like a frog croaking underwater. But any special thing you can do gives you more dimension as a performer — and adds flavor and color to your act."

Robin works hard to keep himself in shape for all of this. "When I was growing up, I was always on all the school teams," he told me. "One year I got four letters. I loved cross-country running, soccer, track, tennis, and wrestling. I did it all in high school. Cross-country running was my favorite. I still love to go way out and run about eight miles. It's wonderful. Nothing beats it."

Robin and his wife Valerie live in an apartment in Los Angeles, which they share with a parrot, two lizards, and an iguana. "One lizard lives in a cage," Robin said. "The other lives under the refrigerator."

What more could anyone ask for? A few short years ago, Robin went to New York with the dream of becoming an actor. Now he's the star of a hit TV show, and he has a booming career, a lovely wife, and a lizard under the refrigerator. He didn't have to become a welder, after all.

I knew I had never met anyone quite like Robin Williams before. But when I first met him, I didn't know that he was going to become a big star — or that *Mork and Mindy* would become the biggest hit of the 1979 TV season.

How had it all happened? To find out, I went back to Los Angeles several months ago to visit the set where the show is produced. I wanted to talk to the people who are in it and the people who are writing and producing it. I wanted to learn all I could about the *Mork and Mindy* story.

Finding A Comedian
Who Could Act

One day a TV writer-producer named Dale McCraven got a telephone call from his friend, Garry Marshall, that was going to affect his life for a long time to come.

"I've known Garry for many years," Dale told me. "He got me in this business, in fact. He said to me: 'Do you want to do a show about a Martian?' And I said, 'I'm sorry. I don't do Martians.'"

Dale smiled. Maybe he doesn't "do" Martians (or write about them), but his friend Garry talked him into coming in to see a *Happy Days* episode that had already been on the air.

"I hadn't seen it," Dale said, "but I agreed to take a look."

Garry Marshall made the same call to another writer-producer named Bruce Johnson. All three men had known each other and worked together over the years. Bruce hadn't seen the episode, either. They seemed to be about the only two people in the whole country who *hadn't* seen it, in fact! For this was the *Happy Days* episode which featured an alien...an alien named Mork, who came from Ork.

The episode had been shown on TV, and the mail began to pour in. "That episode," Bruce Johnson told me later, "received more mail than any other *Happy Days* show."

But since Bruce Johnson and Dale McCraven had not seen it yet, the episode was screened for them after it had been on TV. Garry Marshall had called his two old friends because ABC had asked him to develop a series about Mork, and he needed their help.

Bruce Johnson and Dale McCraven went to see it. "Robin Williams impressed us," they both told me much later. "In that one brief episode, we saw possibilities for a series. We saw Robin himself. And we saw a character with great appeal and great potential."

ABC wanted a series about Mork and Garry Marshall couldn't do it by himself. He was already overseeing four TV shows and writing two plays and two movies. But he could serve as executive producer — and he could turn over the day-to-day development of the series to his two friends; both of them were veteran TV writers and producers.

Dale McCraven and Bruce Johnson agreed to give it a try. Mork wasn't a Martian, after all. He was an Orkan. And *anybody* knows there is a big difference between the two. Dave McCraven had never said he didn't "do" Orkans!

In May 1978, ABC announced plans for a new series about Mork from Ork. They didn't ask for a pilot (or sample) film. They trusted Garry Marshall and the two producers he had hired. Production on the new show was scheduled to begin in July. It would include a young actress under contract to ABC named Pam Dawber. And it would (probably) be called *Mork and Mindy*.

The two producers had their work cut out for them.

"We met one night at Garry's house," Bruce recalled. "We discussed the series and what we might do with it. Dale agreed to write a one-hour show, which was the opening show of the series."

"Why didn't you help him write it?" I asked Bruce, and he smiled.

"I didn't have a pencil," he replied, kiddingly. "So I set up the crews and the cast." He looked at me and then he got serious. "Hiring the crew and the cast is so important. The two of us are the producers. That means we are responsible for everything. If something goes wrong or doesn't work, it's our fault. No one else's. But if we hire the right cast and crew — they make *us* look good. And they have done that on this show."

By June, 1978, Dale was writing the script for the first *Mork and Mindy* show and Bruce was hiring the people to work on it. They were very enthusiastic about the series.

"Do you always feel that way about the show you're working on?" I asked them.

"No," answered Bruce. "But in this case, we felt we had something unusual, something that could take off. It seemed to us that the show had everything. It had a unique talent in Robin Williams. And it had a unique situation that could put that talent to full use."

"Robin Williams," added Dale, "is a very special talent. I can't see him playing a Bob Newhart type of character — someone who goes to work and then comes home to a wife and all kinds of domestic problems. Robin Williams just isn't that kind of person. He couldn't play that kind of character."

But he could play Mork, for Mork isn't like anybody who has ever been on TV. And neither is Robin Williams. Both, it seems, hatched out of the same egg.

"Mork," said Dale, "is like a new-born babe in a grown-up body. He is floundering around in the world. But we all had one concern from the very beginning," the producer added. "We wanted the show to appeal to kids. But not *just* to kids. We wanted it to appeal to everybody. We also didn't want it to be another *My Favorite Martian*. We wanted it to be something different, something broad enough to appeal to young people and to adults."

"It's a strange show," Bruce added. "People see different things in it. They laugh at different things. I watch it with my wife and children. Each of us laughs at different times and at different things. Dale used a term some time ago which we like to think describes *Mork and Mindy*. We like to think of it as being 'intellectual slapstick.' "

The show, the two producers told me, has changed as the weeks have passed. "When we first started," Dale said, "we knew Robin was a funny man but we didn't know if he could act. He can. That has allowed us to put more depth in our scripts. We have five staff writers plus ourselves working on scripts. Bruce and I share writing and producing duties and we do considerable rewriting of other people's scripts."

The subject of script writing brought up an important question about the production of *Mork and Mindy*. I had read in several places that Robin ad-libbed most of his lines. I had also read that the producers left big holes in the scripts so that Robin could ad-lib (or make up his own lines). "Not true," stressed both producers. "A half-hour TV show couldn't possibly be done that way."

"Robin contributes a great deal," Bruce explained. "But we don't leave holes in the scripts! Robin can take lines that have been written and make them sound like ad-libs, which is great. He comes off as being spontaneous, but he is a very studied man. He may try some ad-libs during rehearsals. But when we film the show on Thursday, he knows exactly what he's doing.

"You know," Bruce added, "my 10-year-old son has grown up seeing scripts of TV shows around our house. And yet, he didn't understand until recently that TV shows are written. Actors don't just say whatever comes into their heads.

"The character of Mork has changed a great deal since the series started," Bruce pointed out. "Mork was much more gimmicky in the *Happy Days* episode with his affected walk. He could walk through walls then. We cut down on the gimmicks. If he could walk through walls, he would never be threatened. He could just 'gimmick' his way out of every situation. We didn't want that."

"He was also kind of a villain in *Happy Days*," Dale said. "He was threatening to take an Earthling (Fonzie or Richie) back to Ork. That was all

Yes, it's Mork behind those "shades" and under that furry hat! In this episode, Mork got slightly tipsy on a glass of ginger ale — but Mindy likes him anyway!

right for one show. But when you're doing a series, your leading character has to be a sympathetic character. If he's a villain or a bad guy, viewers aren't going to like him or care about him."

"We took away some of his powers and some of his gimmicks," Bruce told me, "to make him a more rounded character and to make him more vulnerable. He can be hurt now. He can't just walk through a wall to get out of trouble.

"Robin has taken those changes and gone from there. He is very professional in everything he does," the producer added.

So last summer the producers thought they had a hit on their hands in *Mork and Mindy*. Then ABC announced its schedule for the fall. "They scheduled us at 8:00 p.m. ET (Eastern Time) on Mondays," groaned Dale. "That time spot is DEATH because of Monday Night Football. Viewers can't even FIND you until football is over. Only on the East Coast are you seen at 8:00 p.m. The rest of the country carries the football live — and carries you at any other old time, such as 6:00 p.m. on Sunday, when half the TV sets in the country aren't even turned on! A producer can yell and scream, but the network schedule is out of our hands.

"Luckily," Dale said, smiling at the memory, "an executive of ABC came to the filming of three of our shows last summer. He saw the shows and he saw Robin Williams, and he gave us his vote of confidence. Before the season began, the network moved us out of that Monday night time slot. They moved us to Thursdays, where we could rise or fall on our own merits."

And rise it did. By the time I talked to the producers, the series was a hit. "Does it get easier to do the show after it's been on the air awhile?" I asked them.

"In some ways it gets easier," Dale replied, "but in other ways it gets harder. We know the characters better now than we did when we started. But it gets harder to get scripts and to do shows that aren't typical. This is a special show. Robin is a special talent. The scripts must reflect that."

"We've tried to bring a little humanity into the shows," Bruce added. "We don't want to pound viewers on the head, but we try to say what we think is right. We did a good show on nonviolence. Mork's philosophy is that if you hit somebody, everybody is embarrassed for you because you've caused someone pain. And I think we did a nice show on aging and how we treat old people. I don't know if things like that are important to the success of the show, but we think it's important to make some kind of statement."

"Has the popularity of science fiction helped *Mork and Mindy*?" I asked.

Dale said no. "I don't think so," he replied. "I don't believe Mork's popularity is due to his having come from outer space. He could have been raised in the woods by elephants. The important factor is that he is a grown-up child living in a world he doesn't understand.

"When we are trying to come up with ideas for scripts, we can't sit around and talk about our pasts. The writers on *Happy Days* can do that, but we don't have that luxury," Dale said.

"Yes," said Bruce, "that's because only one of us came from Ork."

"And we're not telling which one!" said his partner.

"But in coming up with story ideas, we try to remember emotional things that have happened to us," Bruce explained. "We're working on the Christmas show now. This is Mork's first Christmas; he's like a two-year-old child looking forward to it. Christmas is an emotional experience that most of us can remember and understand. When everybody first read the script of the Christmas show, there were about 30 people in the room. Half of them ended up in tears."

At that moment, the Christmas show was being rehearsed in a studio near the producers' office. I decided it was time to go over and take a look — and meet the other half of the Mork and Mindy team. But before I went to meet Pam Dawber, I asked the two producers what they were going to do after they had finished all the *Mork and Mindy* shows for the first season.

"We've already got our stretchers ordered," Dale answered, looking very serious. I knew he was kidding, though. "They're going to have to carry us out of here. I'm going to New Zealand."

"I'm going to Hawaii," said Bruce.

And neither of them, they assured me, was going in a flying egg.

Shazbot! Mork finds a new way to play the trombone!

Mork Learns About Christmas

Mork and Mindy is filmed before a studio audience on Thursday nights. The people in the show spend the early part of the week learning the many things that go into being in a TV show. They learn their lines, where to stand, and what to do when they are on the stage.

I walked into the studio late one Monday morning. The actors were on a short break. Robin was there, wearing his customary baggy pants with an orange jacket and white shoes. When I walked in, he was dancing around the set, making everyone in the room smile. He stopped when he saw me come in and walked over to where I stood. "Hi!" he said. "You're back! Good to see you!" With that, he flashed a quick smile, and danced away. Then, the director called everyone back to their places. It was time to start rehearsing again. This was the Christmas show they were working on and it was a difficult one, for the theme was very emotional. Everyone wanted it to be done just right.

They were rehearsing in the studio where the show would be filmed on Thursday night. One side of the studio was lined with seven rows of benches covered in a bright-blue material. On Thursday night, these benches would be filled with some 250 lucky fans who had managed to get tickets for the filming. Now, they were empty except for a few scattered onlookers (relatives or friends of the performers). I walked up and took a seat. It didn't take me long to discover that the benches might look pretty, but they were still hard. I knew, though, that no real *Mork and Mindy* fan would mind, for watching the cast of that show at work is quite an experience.

Everything centers around Robin Williams. Robin has moments when he acts like a wacked-out alien, talking backward, singing gibberish, and swinging down from the attic on a rope. The next instant, he'll be standing calmly, listening to the director, and maybe offering some suggestions of his own. He is a master at improvisation; often, during rehearsal, he comes up with lines that are funnier and better than those written by the scriptwriters, and often they are substituted.

"Robin is always trying out new things," a network publicist told me as we sat on our blue benches. "There are times when he is really wild. But he *never* wastes production time. He is too much of a professional to do that. He is always concerned about his fellow actors.

"You know," this same publicist continued, "I went to see his comedy act one night."

"Really?" I replied. "What did you think of it?"

She paused for a moment and then answered. "It was wondrous," she said softly. "When he plays the old man, he is so good it is almost frightening. He *becomes* that old man."

We sat there that morning, watching Robin become Mork — or was it the other way around?

Mork admires a Christmas angel, proudly shown off by Mindy's friend, Susan (Morgan Fairchild). But later in this episode, when Mork tries to make the angel fly — it breaks into a thousand pieces!

Mork was being introduced to Christmas. He was totally confused when he saw his young friend, Eugene, (played by Jeffrey Jacquet) come in to Mindy's apartment carrying a Christmas tree.

"Man," Eugene says to him in disgust, "sometimes you act like you're from another world!"

The director called another brief break in the rehearsal. Robin grabbed Pam Dawber around the waist and swung her around in the air. Then he grabbed a piece of rope and put it around his neck. He pretended to pull it tight, saying, "No more *Mork and Mindy*. Now it's just *Mindy*," and everybody laughed. Then they went back to work.

They had gotten to the final scene, the hardest scene of all. Mork had learned that he was supposed to give Christmas gifts to his friends. But he hadn't quite understood what kind of gifts. Mindy's father and grandmother arrived on Christmas morning. Mork was very excited about the gifts he was giving. Everyone else was horrified by them. His gift to Mindy was something he had created: a bracelet made of dead flies.

"There are lots more upstairs," he told Mindy excitedly, pointing at the flies.

Nobody wanted to tell him the truth. But Mork overheard them talking and realized he had made a terrible mistake. He decided to correct it.

To each one of them, he decided, he would give a thought. This was a very fragile moment.

To Mindy, Mork gave the memory of the time when she had lost a dog that she loved very much. After a long, lonely, horrible week, the dog came home, and it was one of the happiest moments of Mindy's whole life.

To Mindy's grandmother, Mork gave another thought — of the first Christmas she had ever spent with her late husband, when their pockets were empty of money, but their hearts were filled with love.

And to Mindy's father, Mork gave perhaps the most wonderful thought of all, the day he was

It's Mork's first Christmas, and he's really getting into the joy of giving gifts. This one to Mindy is pretty unusual though — it's a bracelet made of dead flies!

Mork calls Eugene (played by Jeffrey Jacquet) his "main munchkin." It's Eugene who clues Mork in on some important Earthling traditions — like Christmas.

presented with a new baby girl who would be called Mindy.

A dry eye in the house? A few, perhaps, but not many, not on any day of the week when that show was being rehearsed and filmed.

As each of the three told about his or her thought, there was absolute silence. Mork stood, knowing somehow that he had learned a lot about Christmas — and maybe taught the others something about it too.

The actors worked hard on the scene. Finally, lunch break was called.

Lunch break? I thought. Not Christmas dinner? Then I realized that it wasn't really time for Christmas dinner. It was time to come back to the realities of a regular working day.

I was going to have lunch with Pam Dawber. I hadn't met Pam before. She walked over to be introduced and suggested that we go to a restaurant near Paramount Studios, where the show was being produced. Pam had one hour — no longer, we were warned — for lunch.

A Girl from Detroit
Meets Mork from Ork

Pam Dawber settled comfortably into the booth of the restaurant near Paramount Studios. "They have *real* mashed potatoes here," she announced, looking around hungrily at what people near us were eating.

"I love to cook," she continued. "I used to cook more than I do now, though. Now I often don't get home from work until 7 or 7:30 at night. So I race out and eat with a friend, or I eat something that's not good for me.

"I never buy frozen vegetables," Pam said. "When I cook, I try to cook whole-grained foods and things that are good for you. Or for me, that is," she added with a laugh. "I'm not a vegetarian. I eat a lot of chicken. But I don't like fish. I'm getting more and more into health foods and vitamins. When I was growing up, my sister and I

46

never drank soda. Our parents wouldn't let us. We drank plain milk and chocolate milk. They tried to get us to drink juice, but I thought that was going too far. I thought that would be too good for us!"

Pam laughed. She is a strikingly pretty, sparkly young woman, who was born in Detroit, Michigan. She began to sing in musical productions when she was in high school in Farmington, Michigan.

"Art and music were my greatest loves in those days," Pam told me. "I had such a good time in high school. I was in all the high school musicals — and I did everything I could to have fun. I wasn't too good a student. I was too busy having a good time."

Pam looked at me and smiled sweetly. "I'd have to admit, I was on the rowdy side," she said. "I was always having to sit in the corner in study hall because I talked too much.

"My choir teacher gave us E's for the day if we talked. When I was in the 12th grade, he said to me, 'You're going to get a D in choir because you have so many E's. But I'll give you a C if you'll try out for the lead in *Kismet*.' I did, and I got the part. Until then I'd been singing and dancing in the choruses!"

Pam didn't take singing lessons until later, but she always loved to sing. "My high school had a wonderful music teacher and a great art department," Pam told me. "We put on very professional shows that were reviewed in the *Detroit News*. There were so many talented kids in that high school. We had three winners in a national art contest, a Miss America candidate... just an incredible group of talented kids.

"Our parents took my sister and me to the theater in Detroit from the time we were very young. They took us to a musical when I was 13. I was *so* in love with the idea of the theater. We bought record albums of all the big musicals. When my parents went out in the evening, I'd sing and dance to the albums and act out all the parts. I'd sing to *Funny Girl*... I'd sing, 'I'm the greatest star and nobody knows it....'"

Talk about dreams, I thought to myself as Pam talked. Here was a person who had sung and danced her heart out as a young girl in her home in Michigan, with not a soul watching or listening. But that hadn't dampened her enthusiasm.

I asked Pam about her sister. "My sister was two and a half years younger than I," Pam replied. "Her name was Leslie. She died three years ago. We were completely different when we were growing up. Our personalities were absolute opposites. I was the aggressive big sister. She was quiet and creative and an excellent art student.

Lovely Pam Dawber plays the role of Mindy McConnell—Mork's best friend on Earth. This rising young star says she really loves working with Robin Williams.

"She was born with a heart defect," Pam continued. "I guess I was jealous because she got more attention than I because of that. I suppose it was fairly typical family rivalry. I wanted a buddy. She wasn't an invalid; she just had a different kind of personality. When we got older, we became closer."

After high school, Pam enrolled in a college in her hometown of Farmington. "It was Oakland Community College," Pam said. "I had decided to go to college to be an artist. But other things began to happen at that same time. The lady next door was a model in Detroit. She asked my mother if I'd be interested in auditioning for the Detroit Auto Show. They wanted a young girl to narrate the show and to introduce a new car called the Firebird.

"I auditioned for the part — and got it! My folks let me do the Detroit show, but they didn't think I should do the show in New York and Chicago. They finally let me, though. So there I was — 17 years old, trying to go to college, and doing auto shows!"

Pam smiled at the memory. "I was having such a good time," she admitted. "My schoolwork began to slip. Then an agent came up to me at one of the auto shows and asked me if I'd be interested in doing print modeling — modeling for catalogues and so on. I said I would be. I finally dropped out of college after the first year. By then, I was traveling all over the country. I really thought I was in show business!

"I went to college," Pam said, "because I wanted to prove to myself that I wasn't dumb. I wanted to get good marks. But I never really enjoyed college. I remember several things that made no sense to me. In one art class, we were drawing and painting and the teacher wouldn't let us talk to our partners. How can you work that way? He said he was going to kick me out of class for talking — and this was in college! That made no sense to me.

"In another class, we were given an assignment very early in the year to do a paper on 'Who Am I?' I worked so hard on that paper — and I got a B minus on it. I was heartbroken. So I hung on to the paper. At the end of the year, I changed the title of the paper to 'What Am I?' and made a couple of small changes in it, and turned it in again. That time I got an A. And it was the same paper! That really made me ask myself what I was doing in college."

After she quit college, Pam kept busy doing auto shows and print modeling. Then, in 1971, she went to a family wedding in Pennsylvania. "At that same time," Pam recalled, "a girlfriend of mine was visiting her father in New York. I went there to see her. She suggested, as a lark, that we go to a model agency and see if they'd take us. We went to one of the major agencies and they took me. My friend was too short. I went back to Detroit and told my parents I wanted to move to New York. They didn't try to stop me. They were very supportive, in fact. I was 19 then."

It was a big step to take, but Pam knew one woman who lived in New York. "I had met her doing the auto shows," Pam told me. "She had been the makeup woman and had been like a guardian to the kids in the group. I called her and said I was coming to New York. She said I could stay with her for a couple of weeks. I ended up living there for more than a year. Then I got my own place. She was a good friend to have," Pam added. "And she knew lots of show business people!"

Pam enjoyed those early years in New York, she told me. "I was very lucky," she said. "I started doing catalogue work right away. Ward's was my biggest client. I also did Sears and other stores. And I did makeup ads and so on. New York seemed so exciting to me then. It was one adventure after another!"

But then the novelty wore off. Pam was working hard, but, somehow....

"I got lonely and I got fat," she told me. "I was eating all kinds of food that wasn't good for me. I didn't have many friends, so I'd sit home and go on eating binges. I'd eat a whole container of ice cream and big globs of cake. Then, for days, I'd live on coffee and grapefruit. I got my system all goofed up.

"I became more and more depressed. My eating habits were so bad, and my body was in terrible shape. My sister became sick, and several of my relatives died. Then I was dropped by my boyfriend...."

Pam sighed as she told me all this during our luncheon interview. Her life had changed considerably since then, but she hadn't forgotten those bad days.

She continued the story of her life in New York. "I was taking voice lessons and acting classes. I was doing a package design for a coffee company. I was modeling, acting, suffering over my lost boyfriend....

"Every time I went on an audition for an acting job, I blew it because I was too nervous. I tried out mainly for musicals, but I tried out for several dramas too. Sometimes I got called back and I'd think maybe I was going to get the job. But I never did.

"I had been in New York for four years by that time," Pam continued. "I was tired of modeling. I was tired of doing the same old thing over and over again."

But then came the turning point. The head of the modeling agency where Pam worked was married to a man who booked talent for a TV talk show. "I finally decided to ask him to listen to me sing," Pam told me. "He agreed to listen. At that same time, his wife was putting together a big show. She was going to send all her best models out on the road to give crash courses to would-be models and their teachers all over the country. I was picked as one of those models. We would go to different cities and teach modeling teachers and their students. At the end of the course in each city, we would have a big banquet. This woman's husband hired me to sing at these banquets! At first, I was terrified. Sometimes there were 400 people there! But I did it and I kept doing it. And I became less and less nervous.

"I sang at banquets in Los Angeles, San Francisco, Seattle. . . . Then I went back to New York and tried out for a leading part in a musical — and got it!"

It was her first professional role and it was a good one. It was the part of the sister, Jennie, in *Sweet Adeline* at the Goodspeed Opera House in East Haddam, Connecticut.

"And that got the whole ball rolling," Pam exclaimed. "It gave me confidence. The same week I got that part, I auditioned for a new ABC series called *Tabitha*. ABC flew me to California to screen test for *Tabitha*. I didn't get that part, but I was one of the two finalists — and that was the closest I'd ever come to getting a role in a TV show. Then I flew directly from California to Connecticut to play the part in *Sweet Adeline*."

As so often happens, things began to happen fast. Suddenly, Pam didn't need (or want!) to eat globs of ice cream and cake to ease her loneliness and unhappiness. While she was in California, she had also gone to meet movie producer Robert Altman's casting director. Altman was doing a movie then that had already been cast. But his casting director remembered Pam.

One day while she was appearing in *Sweet Adeline* in Connecticut, Pam made a quick trip into her apartment in New York City. While she was there, the phone rang. It was Robert Altman's casting director. Altman was in town for one day. He wanted to meet Pam.

"I walked into his apartment," Pam remembered, "and he said, 'Do you know how to ride a horse?' I said, 'Sure.' He said, 'Good.' "

That's all there was to it. Altman offered Pam a role in his upcoming film, *A Wedding*. She accepted.

"*Sweet Adeline* closed in Connecticut on a Saturday," Pam said. "I went home to my apartment in New York, did my laundry, packed, and flew to Chicago on Sunday. The movie was

55

filmed outside of Chicago. I spent two and a half months there. It was a wonderful learning experience. I knew nothing about doing movies. I thought it would be like doing one big TV commercial. But it *wasn't*."

During her years in New York, Pam did one thing that she is forever grateful for. "I saved my money and bought a cabin on the Delaware River in upstate New York," she told me. "It overlooks cornfields and mountains and water. When I'm there, I cook big dinners for friends who live nearby or who come up from the city. That's the kind of cooking I love. I make up recipes as I go along."

Pam loves that cabin. It is her refuge. After she finished the Robert Altman movie, she went there to rest and relax. Then she headed back to New York. "I figured, 'Now I'm going to be a movie star!' she told me with a rueful laugh. "But I wasn't."

She had given up modeling, but no better offers came along. "So I started modeling again," she said.

But ABC had been keeping an eye on this young actress-singer-model. She hadn't gotten the part in *Tabitha*, but the network had been impressed by her screen test. Finally, they offered her a contract. They were willing to pay her a regular salary until they could find the right part for her.

"It was a good contract," Pam said. "It said that I couldn't do a series for any other network, but it didn't prevent me from doing other things. And it gave me the right to read scripts and see if I wanted to do them.

"I read…maybe five scripts. Then I agreed to do *Sister Terri*. That was a comedy about a nun. I didn't think it would sell, or be made into a series, but I knew that doing it would be a good experience for me."

Pam did a *Sister Terri* pilot film in May 1978. After that, I went to Hawaii and then to my cabin

It's not easy teaching an Orkan what's what on Earth! Here, Mindy has just sent Mork to the attic to get a comforter — but he's brought down a deer head and a horn! "Which one is the comforter?" he seems to be asking.

in upstate New York," Pam recalled. "Two weeks later my agent called me at my cabin and said, 'ABC and Paramount like you.' That was on a Friday. The following Monday, my agent called and said, 'Listen to this.' He read from a trade paper: 'Robin Williams and Pam Dawber will star in a new series called *Mork and Mindy*.' Robin didn't know, I didn't know, my agent didn't know. There had been no auditions...."

Pam smiled. "I said to my agent, 'What is *Mork and Mindy*? It sounds pretty stupid to me!' I was flattered," Pam admitted, "but I was a little upset because they hadn't asked me if I wanted to do it.

"Then," said Pam, "they sent me a tape of Robin playing Mork in *Happy Days*. And I thought—wow!—he's something special. Soon after that, I had lunch with Garry Marshall in New York. He said that the show would be built around Robin and that we would all be free to add our own thoughts and ideas. On that basis, I agreed to do it. I didn't meet Robin until a month before the show went into production."

Once she met Robin, and began to work with him, Pam discovered something. "Being in this show is so much fun," she said. "We play all day. Robin is a *joy*. I look forward to coming to work! Everybody on the show has formed such a happy group. Robin's attitude has affected us all. No one who is involved with the show—the producers, the writers, the actors—feels he is more important than anyone else.

"Robin is the main energy of our show. Obviously, he is the star of the show. And there are times when he doesn't follow the script. He improvises," Pam noted. "When he does that, all I can do is stay loose. I remind myself: 'I'm here because I'm having a good time.' And I tell myself before I go out in front of the studio audience that if I blow a line, we'll all laugh, and so will the studio audience."

Pam is thrilled with the success of *Mork and Mindy*, for herself, for all the people on the show, and for her parents.

"After the death of my sister," Pam told me, "there was such a hole in our family. How do parents ever get over something like that? But then this show came along and it is so big and so wonderful—it has helped my parents.

"They have become neighborhood celebrities, now. Little kids come by the house and stand there and point. It's wonderful!" Pam paused and smiled.

"You know," she added, "when I used to sing as a kid, my parents always thought I was wonderful, but they didn't pay too much attention. Who would? After I had gone to New York, my

**Believe it or not — this is how Mork first sat in a chair!
Mindy's convinced it's easy — if you have just come from
Ork!**

mother said, 'We always thought you had a nice voice, but you're our daughter. We didn't really *know*.'"

Pam laughed fondly. Then she thought for a moment about success. "I'm a strong believer in one thing," she said. "I don't ever want to have everything. The quickest way to unhappiness is to buy everything. Then nothing is special. People buy and buy and buy. Then they find there is a hole they can't fill no matter how much they buy. They find that money and material possessions can't fill that hole."

Our interview was over, and it was time for Pam to get back to work. Many young actresses might have been jealous over the success of Robin and his portrayal of Mork. Pam wasn't, and that is much to her credit. She shares in the success of the show, and she knows how to share it without being temperamental.

Mindy had taken in an alien called Mork. And Pam wasn't about to be any less gracious than her TV counterpart.

From Football in the Living Room to an Alien in the Attic

Mindy's father didn't know at first that Mork was an alien. He just thought Mork was strange...*very* strange. Finally, he had to be told, and he took the news well, especially for an older, rather conservative Earthling. He hated to admit it, but he'd grown rather fond of Mork, of his backward expressions and weird behavior.

Mindy's father, Frederick McConnell, is played by Conrad Janis, a man who has been a professional actor since he was 13 years old. Back in those days, when he was a teenager, he didn't plan on being an actor. He planned on being a baseball player. But Conrad Janis got a part in a play — and just kept on getting parts.

I had lunch with Conrad one day during my visit to the *Mork and Mindy* set. When lunch break was called, Conrad picked up his trombone, tucked it safely into its case, and off we went. The waitress didn't even look surprised when we came marching...er, walking, into the restaurant. Conrad put his trombone down carefully and offered me a seat.

Clearly, he wasn't going to say a word about the trombone. When I asked, he explained with a smile. "I take it to work with me so that I can practice during the day whenever I have any free time," he said. "Tonight I'm playing in a jam session with a band I work with."

Conrad grew up in New York City. "I went to private schools there," he told me. "And the day I graduated from the eighth grade, a boy in my class said to me: 'I'm going to go audition for a play. Why don't you come with me?' Well," said Conrad, remembering that day, "I had always played the lead in all the school plays, so I thought, 'Why not?' So I went with him. The play was a Broadway production of *Junior Miss*, directed by Moss Hart.

"When we got there, there was a long line. There must have been 450 of us. They marched us through in groups of six. And then they asked 50 of us to come back and read. Then six of us were picked. Some of the people in the original group were as old as 30. I was 13. I was a teenager, which is what they were casting."

Conrad got the part in the play. Then he told his parents. "I walked home," he recalled, "and said, 'Guess what....' I ended up being in *Junior Miss* on Broadway and then in road show productions of it. I was in the play for three years.

"My parents always encouraged me to do whatever I wanted to do. My whole family was always committed to the arts," Conrad added. "My parents wrote books on art. They were also well-known collectors of 20th Century art. Now my father and my brother, Carroll, run the Sidney Janis Gallery in New York, a gallery which has revolutionized the way art is shown in galleries around the world."

But young Conrad took to acting more than he did to art. "Acting to me was a neat way to get out of going to school," he admitted. "I went to private school when I was doing *Junior Miss* on Broadway. When we took the show on the road, I took correspondence courses. It was hard to pay much attention to them, though. There were too many other things going on that were more interesting.

"I was 16 when I came back from doing *Junior Miss* on the road," Conrad said. "I had been away from regular school for too long. So I quit school and got myself into another Broadway play."

He was fast on his way to becoming a teenage

Conrad Janis plays Mindy's dad, Frederick J. McConnell. Conrad says he's tried to make the character of Mindy's father more sympathetic toward Mork than it was in the beginning.

star. Then, Hollywood beckoned, so Conrad headed for California. "I was put under contract to 20th Century-Fox," he said. "They paid me a good salary, even though I only did a couple of pictures a year for them. That meant I had a lot of spare time. They made most young performers go to acting school. But since I had been on Broadway, they figured I knew how to act.

"At that time," Conrad explained, "there were a lot of fine jazz musicians in Los Angeles, many of whom had worked in New Orleans. I fell in love with the music and the sounds of jazz. I was 18, but I had to lie about my age to get in the places where many of these people played. Finally, I bought myself a trombone and tried to copy the sounds I was hearing. I didn't take formal lessons until later."

Conrad always managed to keep busy, he said. "There were never any really long stretches when I wasn't working," he told me. "But I had my ups and downs as a teenage actor. I went through some difficult times trying to adjust. It isn't easy at any age, but I think it's especially hard when you're young. I went through periods when I was very popular, and periods when I wasn't."

Conrad spent a lot of time traveling back and forth between the East Coast and the West Coast, doing plays, doing movies, and playing his trombone.

"Early in the 1950's, I started doing live TV in New York. What an experience!" he said enthusiastically. "I was in more than 200 live shows — *Studio One, Suspense, Philco Playhouse* — all of them! I loved working in TV then. There is nothing like going on the air *live*."

But despite his long career, Conrad admitted that he has never been in anything quite like *Mork and Mindy*. "Being on the show is a fantastically lucky break for me," he said. "I love the show and the people in it. I got the part because I had played the father of a teenage girl on an episode of *Happy Days* — and the producers remembered me when they were casting *Mork and Mindy*. I figured from the very beginning that the show was going to be a big hit.

"Robin Williams is a new kind of comedian," Conrad pointed out. "He is very funny and very fresh, and I think they've come up with a format that gives him freedom to express what he is as a person and as an actor. When he plays Mork, we see ourselves through new eyes. We can't lie to Mork, and that makes us examine ourselves and what we are really like.

"We kid around a lot on the set," Conrad added with a smile. "Robin loves to improvise.

Sometimes, when we're kidding around, he's actually trying out new ideas for the show. Often, on the spur of the moment, he comes up with a funnier joke in rehearsal than the one that had been written.

"The other people on the show," Conrad said, "have to be ready to respond. Robin keeps us on our toes. If he changes a line of dialogue, we have to respond to it. I've never worked in a show like this," the veteran actor said. "Robin is very imaginative."

When the series first began, Conrad was not satisfied with one thing about it. The character he was playing, he believed, wasn't quite right. He explained why:

"Mindy, you know, has moved out of her father's home into her own apartment," Conrad said. "At first, her father was furious that she had left him. He was very moralistic and preachy and kind of pompous.

"But Pam plays her part so sympathetically, and so does Robin, that her father would have to be a beast to dislike Mork — or to dislike Mindy's newly-found freedom. On my own, I began to change the character. When I had to say lines that were nasty to Mork, I said them in a way that wasn't nasty. I switched the character around completely to someone who is much more loving and understanding than he was at first.

"Obviously," Conrad remarked, "the producers saw what I was doing. But nobody ever told me not to do it or to play the character another way. The producers check everything very carefully — including the response to every show and every character. If they hadn't liked what I was doing, they would have said so."

Clearly, the producers did like the change, and Mindy's father has remained a kinder, more sympathetic character.

"Very few actors get a chance to do a show like this," Conrad told me as we finished lunch and began to walk back to the set. "But I have been in this business long enough to know that strange things happen. There are never any guarantees. You have to enjoy what you are doing today and not worry about tomorrow. I'm here now and I'm thrilled to be working in this show. I will never understand," Conrad continued, "why actors quit TV series. It's too hard to get work!"

Since Conrad has been busy working ever since he was 13 years old, I asked him, "Didn't you miss some of the fun of being a teenager?" He shook his head vigorously.

"Not at all!" he exclaimed. "I never felt I missed anything! I had lots of friends. My brother and I played ball all the time. I figured that was really the life — to play ball all day and work at night. We used to play football in the living room. We didn't know or care that there were priceless paintings on the walls. My father finally gave his art collection to the Museum of Modern Art. We had stopped playing football in the living room by that time.

"As a kid, I thought art was boring, sissy stuff. But I guess it rubbed off on me. I have a collection of paintings which are in storage in New York at the moment. I'm renting a house here in Los Angeles which is totally different from any other place I've ever lived. I grew up in an apartment filled with 20th Century art and furniture. This house I'm renting is filled with wonderfully comfortable traditional furniture and big leather chairs. I love it."

Watch out Mr. McConnell — there's a strange-looking Orkan slowly creeping up on you!

After we left the restaurant, I was having trouble keeping up with Conrad. He was walking and talking fast. "Don't you ever get tired?" I gasped. We had been through acting, art, music, furniture...and Conrad was still going strong.

"I've always been very energetic," he replied in one of the biggest understatements of the day. "But once I was in the play, *Same Time Next Year*. Only two people are in the play and we were on stage all the time. I was in it for about a year. When it was over, I went and collapsed in a hammock for three weeks."

"Ha!" I thought to myself, he wears down just like the rest of us. Then I looked over at him and I wasn't so sure. I could tell what he was thinking by the cheerful look on his face. If he walked faster, maybe he'd have time to play his trombone for a little while, he was thinking. And he began to walk faster.

A Kind of Magic Takes Over

My days on the set of *Mork and Mindy* went by very quickly. The Christmas show took shape as I sat and watched. Robin was always there, talking and laughing and entertaining everyone around.

Months ago, when Mork stepped out of that big white egg, nobody knew that *Mork and Mindy* would become one of the biggest hits of the year. The fact that it did is a credit to everyone involved. I had spent the past few days talking to those people, and one thing was clear. When an idea works, a kind of magic takes over, and all the pieces fall into place.

On *Mork and Mindy,* the magic begins with Robin, but it doesn't end there. It extends to all the people on the show.

Mork arrived on our planet and understood

Mork and Mindy shake hands — Orkan style!

very little of what he saw. He moved into Mindy's attic and set up an apartment. And he was very proud of it. "It's scab city," he boasted. "It's totally taste-free."

Almost everyone Mork ran into thought he was bonkers. TV viewers agreed. "This show is so crazy," said one viewer, "it will probably be a big hit."

Millions of us laughed and giggled as Mork ate flowers and sat on his head and talked backwards. But then we began to realize something. Mork was looking at us Earthlings through the eyes of a total stranger. He was seeing us as we really are. And, often, the craziness we were laughing at wasn't his at all. It was ours!

Robin is a free spirit. He is also a trained, disciplined, thinking actor. In playing Mork, he has created a character who makes us laugh and cry and care. That's what TV hits are all about.

Mork stepped out of that big white egg and was told not to get involved. But he did, and so did we. I left the Mork and Mindy set, knowing I had shared a special time with a very special group of people.

Two friends share a joke — and a glass of milk. Learning the strange ways of Earthlings is much easier for Mork with Mindy there to help him.